Order in the House of God

Merica Cox

JER 8:22
BALM OF GILEAD
WORLD MINISTRIES

CGW
PUBLISHING

2016

Order in the House of God

First Edition: August 2016

ISBN 978-1-908293-06-0

Published by:

CGW Publishing
B 1502
PO Box 15113
Birmingham
B2 2NJ
United Kingdom

www.cgwpublishing.com

mail@cgwpublishing.com

Contents

ORDER IN THE HOUSE OF GOD

In my journeys as a minister I have seen the lack of order in the charismatic churches. Believers are empowered and excited to do ministry but lack direction and guidance resulting in chaos. Sometimes you hear such sentiments like, "God is not afraid of noise" etc. The truth of the matter however is that God is not the author of chaos but rather a God of order. God has principles and a pattern of how his work should be carried out with excellency and dignity fit for a King of Kings.

An example of chaos is when demons manifest in church and people run from their seats and start shouting come out, come out. This can be frightening for visitors or children in the congregation. Also when people are being prayed for at the altar the believers in the congregation running to the front to pray for people randomly, this experience can be frightening for some people. I remember years back when I was invited to a Pentecostal church, I was coming from a Seventh Day Adventist background. I was touched by the word being preached and responded to an altar call; before I knew what was happening there was a group of people surrounding me screaming "cry if you want to cry" etc., etc.

I was not able to hear what the spirit was saying to me, I was focusing on what the people were doing and saying, the whole thing turned into a nightmare. The first opportunity I got I ran out of that church and I never returned there, it took four years before I could go to another Pentecostal church again.

There is another issue concerning our liberty in worship, sometimes saints become so excited and the service quickly turns into a semi nightclub. The dances become very sensual and disturbing; you can see the flesh completely taking over. Sometimes one needs to stop and assess the scene then ask yourself how does God view this scene, is for God or is it for our own pleasure. Does this glorify God, is it pleasing to him?

Someone will say, "Ah, what about King David who danced shamelessly before the

Lord?", this misunderstanding is perhaps due to lack of knowledge, there was no confusion in his dancing as it was time of celebration and everyone danced as if in a wedding precession so this was acceptable accept by his wife who despised him. David's wife had her own personal reasons for this; we also need to understand this came from a heart full of pride, bitterness and envy if you follow her story. The bible does not say David danced in sensual way, when he danced before the Lord his thoughts were centred on God alone and not on humans and that makes a difference. David knew the God of Israel and would not have dared to bring strange fire before the lord especially after the death of Uzzah.

Order is of paramount importance to God, people often speak of organized chaos; this means those involved see nothing wrong as everything is planned yet in reality it is still chaos. Chaos in charismatic circles often puts people off these meetings and those who attend are often carried away with emotionalism and very little spiritual growth is gained.

Chaos also opens a door to occultism, demons love a chaotic environment as this affords them an opportunity to pretend to be the work of the holy spirit. Many times people are deceived into thinking these chaotic manifestations are the work of the holy spirit.

In one meeting a lady stated started praying in tongues, she got louder and louder, I asked everyone to be silent but she kept on. I knew this was a demon, you see self-control is the fruit of the spirit but the demons have no self-control. So I rebuked the demon in the name of Jesus, everyone was horrified as they thought I had made a mistake, just then the demon manifested and she started cursing and swearing. People were confused because she had been speaking in tongues, demons are copy cats, they use camouflage to remain undetected.

Self-control can be the determining factor as to whether the manifestation is of God or not. 1Co 14:32 "And the spirits of the prophets are subject to the prophets".

The Apostle Paul who was a master builder

was concerned about the order in the church.

1Co 14:26-33 "How is it then, brethren? when ye come together, every one of you hath a psalm, hath a doctrine, hath a tongue, hath a revelation, hath an interpretation. Let all things be done unto edifying. If any man speak in an unknown tongue, let it be by two, or at the most by three, and that by course; and let one interpret. But if there be no interpreter, let him keep silence in the church; and let him speak to himself, and to God. Let the prophets speak two or three, and let the other judge. If anything be revealed to another that sitteth by, let the first hold his peace. For ye may all prophesy one by one, that all may learn, and all may be comforted. And the spirits of the prophets are subject to the prophets. For God is not the author of confusion, but of peace, as in all churches of the saints.".

1Co 14:40 "Let all things be done decently and in order".

Women are emotional beings and can be very vocal, not knowing when to be quiet and when to speak. The sort of chaos within the Corinthian church still exists in churches today where there is a lack of teaching.

Paul taught order in worship services and order in partaking of Holy Communion (table of the Lord) 1Co 14:34 "Let your women keep silence in the churches: for it is not permitted unto them to speak; but they are commanded to be under obedience, as also saith the law." 1Co 14:35 "And if they will learn anything, let them ask their husbands at home: for it is a shame for women to speak in the church".

God has a plan for his church, it is this plan which Jesus taught to the Apostles and told them to pass it on to all generations. God gave instructions to Moses:

Exo 25:8 "And let them make me a sanctuary; that I may dwell among them."

Exo 25:9 "According to all that I shew thee, after the pattern of the tabernacle, and the pattern of all the instruments thereof, even so shall ye make it".

Exo 40:33b "So Moses finished the work." (Then God inspected it)

Exo 40:34 "Then a cloud covered the tent of the congregation, and the glory of the LORD filled the tabernacle. Exo 40:35 And Moses was not able to enter into the tent of the congregation, because the cloud abode thereon, and the glory of the LORD filled the tabernacle".

Again we see Solomon the son of David, he built a house for God according to the instructions given to him by his father David. Solomon put everything in this temple which God had commanded Moses to do. This was restoration of everything God had put in the Tebanacle of Moses. The bible tells us:

1Ki 8:10 "And it came to pass, when the priests were come out of the holy place, that The cloud filled the house of the LORD, 1Ki 8:11 So that the priests could not stand to minister because of the cloud: for the glory of the LORD had filled the house of the LORD".

Reading the above scriptures causes one to

understand that God is a God of Order and will not dwell where there is dis-order. God is a God of principles, he works through a planned process, anyone who wishes to please God must do things God's way.

Pro 16:25 "There is a way that seemeth right unto a man, but the end thereof are the ways of death."

God has three priorities and they are found in Rev 11:1 "And there was given me a reed like unto a rod: and the angel stood, saying, Rise, and measure the temple of God, and the altar, and them that worship therein."

I am reminded of Noah, when God asked him to build an Ark he had not seen any rain, his protection and that of his family and all that God had entrusted into his hand depended on his obedience in carrying out God's instruction about building the Ark.

Obedience is better that sacrifice. If Noah had compromised the instructions given him the Ark (boat) would have sunk.

There are three areas which are very

important to the Lord; focusing on only one or two will cause imbalance of these areas. What concerns God must concern us; mature growth involves a balanced rounded growth. Remember one of the principles is, "as it is in the natural so it is in the spiritual". Can you imagine a child growing up, only their arms are growing or only their head is growing, we would term the child disabled. So when a church or organisation fails to teach a balanced word of God they are disabling the people. God measures the Temple (church structure, the Altar, prayer, giving and worship life of the church) and the Worshippers (members of the church and congregation).

We need to understand that there is a full dimension in the Word and we must enter into it. Apostasy (falling away from truth) can involve bringing of the Word down to our size. This means fitting the Word in what we are doing rather than us fitting into the Word. Let us look at these priorities as revealed to John by the Lord Jesus in Revelation 11:1.

1. MEASURE THE TEMPLE

God desires the church to be strong and well built, to be structured right according to Gods standards. God wants everything to be in its proper place (order), build according to his plan and his purposes.

Remember we are dealing with lives, eternal souls, therefore we can't afford to be wrong or do things anyhow. Gods desire is for the church to be strong, solid, safe and secure. Imagine Noah's Ark(boat), no one has seen rain in those days and therefore Noah had to follow God's instructions carefully, the boat would unfortunately be tested only when it was already in the water. If the boat was not built right or if Noah took short cuts it would fail the test, its failure would be catastrophic as everything in it would be lost. In the same way a church or organization is a boat carrying people to safety, its failure means the loss of internal life.

What should the structure look like?

- Senior minister (manifesting Christ's headship)

- Multiple ministry not multiple authority(submission)

- Every function or ministry department must be under covering – oversight

- An order of becoming a member (how one is planted)

- An order of how one is recognised and released in ministry

- Governmental procedure must agree with the word

- Each person must know their job description e.g. Elders, deacons and fivefold ministry

The ultimate goal is for the Temple to be filled with God's presence, life and his glory; for the river of Christ life to flow out of the Temple to reach the world.

2. MEASURE THE ALTAR

The Altar is a place of meeting with God, our relationship with him. God wants us to measure our Altar and see what size it is.

The church need to make certain that people are getting through to God, they are being truly born again. Church should ensure people are coming in via the DOOR which is Christ Jesus, this is ensuring there is a strong foundation being laid in people's lives.

1. Repentance involves one's heart, mind and will.

2. Water baptism is entered in with faith calling on the name of the Lord for change and that there is a cutting off of the old nature through hear circumcision and burial of the old man.

3. Holy Spirit baptism with the evidence of speaking in tongues, a river flowing out of one's innermost being.

We lay our lives at the Altar as living sacrifices because of his grace and love. When people respond to the altar call there should be little interference or disturbance to enable the Holy Spirit to do a deep work in the hearts of people. Too often the Spirit is not given room to operate as zealous and uninformed saints with good intentions interfere with God's dealing with man.

The Altar also speaks of an individual's prayer life, laying hold of God through intercession, travail and fastings. Having the desire to see people turn to God and being transformed.

The Altar is where we bring our gifts of self, service and substance to God, this involves tithes, offerings and giving regularly and liberally. At the Altar we also remember our relationships with others, we forgive and release those who have hurt us as God has forgiven us.

We must measure our Altar to see if it is up to the standard of God's word. Remember the Word or God is our measuring rod not man's opinion or rules.

3. MEASURE THE WORSHIPPERS

God is very interested in our worship, there are over 350 teaching verses on worship in the bible. Jesus speaking to the Samaritan woman in John 4 said that the true worshippers will worship the father in truth and in spirit. God dwells in the praises of his people.

Worship is the result of having a new covenant heart of flesh.

Deu 30:6 "And the LORD thy God will circumcise thine heart, and the heart of thy seed, to love the LORD thy God with all thine heart, and with all thy soul, that thou mayest live".

Php 3:3 "For we are the circumcision, which worship God in the spirit, and rejoice in Christ Jesus, and have no confidence in the flesh".

Psa 50:23 "Whoso offereth praise glorifieth me: and to him that ordereth his conversation aright will I shew the salvation of God".

Psa 22:3 "But thou art holy, O thou that inhabitest the praises of Israel".

1. Worship in spirit – through the new created spirit

2. Worship in truth – according to the word and sincerity from the heart

3. Worship in joy and liberty

4. Worship with Psalms, hymns and spiritual songs

Be a worshipper, be a worshipping church and remember God looks in the heart and that's where the measurement is taken. How big is your heart of worship towards God?

We must measure every activity we do in the name of Christ using the Word of God. We must preach, teach the whole gospel according to the Apostles. We must prayerfully confirm people into ministry because they have a genuine call of God and have been proven and are under submission not because they are charismatic and busy bodies. God always moves to confirm his word and to encourage his people. Where the genuine word is preached or taught there comes a freshness and quality of life to the congregation.

The Temple, Altar and Worship must all be balanced; and in line with the word of God. We must respond positively to God's challenge and His priorities. We must resolve to measure up to God's standard for the Temple, Altar and worship. We must be prepared and committed to make any adjustments that are necessary.

Remember the Word of God says that if we Judge(measure) ourselves we will not be judged. 1Co 11:31 "For if we would judge ourselves, we should not be judged."

1Co 11:32 "But when we are judged, we are chastened of the Lord, that we should not be condemned with the world".

Joh 12:48 "He that rejecteth me, and receiveth not my words, hath one that judgeth him: the word that I have spoken, the same shall judge him in the last day".

DOING THINGS GOD'S WAY

David desired to bring the Ark of God from amongst the Philistines, this was a good and honourable thing to do.

2Sa 6:2 "And David arose, and went with all the people that were with him from Baale of Judah, to bring up from thence the ark of God, whose name is called by the name of the LORD of hosts that dwelleth between the cherubims. 2Sa 6:3 And they set the ark of God upon a new cart, and brought it out of the house of Abinadab that was in Gibeah: and Uzzah and Ahio, the sons of Abinadab, drave the new cart. 2Sa 6:4 And they brought it out of the house of Abinadab which was at Gibeah, accompanying the ark of God: and Ahio went before the ark. 2Sa 6:5 And David and all the house of Israel played before the LORD on all manner of instruments made of fir wood, even on harps, and on psalteries, and on timbrels, and on cornets, and on cymbals. 2Sa 6:6 And when they came to Nachon's threshing floor, Uzzah put forth his hand to the ark of God, and took hold of it; for the oxen shook it. 2Sa 6:7 And the anger of the LORD was kindled against Uzzah; and God smote him there for his error; and there he died by the ark of God".

David's desire was right but due to ignorance or shall we say neglect of God's principles his effort only brought death. David was upset with God not understanding why Uzzah died. David later discovered that he had used the methods of the Philistines rather than God's ordained order of carrying the Ark. So David repented and went about doing things God's way, David followed the instructions and gladly brought the Ark home with singing and dancing.

Considering Uzzah, the ark of God had been with Uzzah's father for many years; Uzzah should have known better than to touch the Ark of God. Familiarity breeds contempt, when people get too familiar with God's presence the fear of God departs from them. The fear of the Lord is the beginning of wisdom, many Christians today lack wisdom. The bible says fools tread where angels fear.

David Loved the Lord so much, no wonder

God called him, "the man after my heart". David desired to build a house for his God, this time however he talked to God about his desire first. Listen to the conversation between David and his Son Solomon.

1Ch 22:7" And David said to Solomon, My son, as for me, it was in my mind to build an house unto the name of the LORD my God: 1Ch 22:8 But the word of the LORD came to me, saying, Thou hast shed blood abundantly, and hast made great wars: thou shalt not build an house unto my name, because thou hast shed much blood upon the earth in my sight. 1Ch 22:9 Behold, a son shall be born to thee, who shall be a man of rest; and I will give him rest from all his enemies round about: for his name shall be Solomon, and I will give peace and quietness unto Israel in his days. 1Ch 22:10 He shall build an house for my name; and he shall be my son, and I will be his father; and I will establish the throne of his kingdom over Israel for ever. 1Ch 22:11 Now, my son, the LORD be with thee; and prosper thou, and build the house of the LORD thy God, as he hath said of thee".

Can you imagine what would have happened had David presumptuously build the house;

God would have rejected the house, all the years of building, all the resources wasted and the crushing feeling of rejection. Have you ever wondered why Jesus spoke these words;

Mat 7:21 " Not every one that saith unto me, Lord, Lord, shall enter into the kingdom of heaven; but he that doeth the will of my Father which is in heaven. Mat 7:22 Many will say to me in that day, Lord, Lord, have we not prophesied in thy name? and in thy name have cast out devils? And in thy name done many wonderful works? Mat 7:23 And then will I profess unto them, I never knew you: depart from me, ye that work iniquity".

Every time I read this scripture I tremble realising that it's not what I do for the Lord but rather being obedient to his will and his ways. As you can see God is a God of principles, everything he does has a purpose is therefore measured precisely for that purpose.

Part of testing for Christians is in the area of obedience, are you able to follow

Instructions without deviating. A servant must learn to follow his master's instructions whole heartedly, they should not assume anything but rather ask if not sure.

Jesus warned; "Strive to enter in at the strait gate: for many, I say unto you, will seek to enter in, and shall not be able. When once the master of the house is risen up, and hath shut the door, and ye begin to stand without, and to knock at the door, saying, Lord, Lord, open unto us; and he shall answer and say unto you, I know you not whence ye are: Then shall ye begin to say, We have eaten and drunk in thy presence, and thou hast taught in our streets. But he shall say, I tell you, I know you not whence ye are; depart from me, all ye workers of iniquity.

There shall be weeping and gnashing of teeth, when ye shall see Abraham, and Isaac, and Jacob, and all the prophets, in the kingdom of God, and you yourselves thrust out". (Luk 13:24-28).

Again Jesus warned; "Then shall the kingdom of heaven be likened unto ten virgins, which took their lamps, and went forth to meet the bridegroom.

And five of them were wise, and five were foolish. They that were foolish took their lamps, and took no oil with them: But the wise took oil in their vessels with their lamps.

While the bridegroom tarried, they all slumbered and slept. And at midnight there was a cry made.

Behold, the bridegroom cometh; go ye out to meet him. Then all those virgins arose, and trimmed their lamps. And the foolish said unto the wise, Give us of your oil; for our lamps are gone out. But the wise answered, saying, Not so; lest there be not enough for us and you: but go ye rather to them that sell, and buy for yourselves.

And while they went to buy, the bridegroom came; and they that were ready went in with him to the marriage: and the door was shut. Afterward came also the other virgins, saying, Lord, Lord, open to us. But he answered and said, Verily I say unto you, I know you not. Watch therefore, for ye know neither the day nor the hour wherein the Son of man cometh". (Mat 25:1-13).

Pro 2:10-11 "When wisdom entereth into thine heart, and knowledge is pleasant unto thy soul; Discretion shall preserve thee, understanding shall keep thee."

Pro 1:5 "A wise man will hear, and will increase learning; and a man of understanding shall attain unto wise counsels."

Pro 1:7 "The fear of the LORD is the beginning of knowledge: but fools despise wisdom and instruction."

Order in the House of God

MINISTRY OF LAYING ON OF HANDS

There are five functions for the ministry of laying on of hands:

1. Impartation

2. Identification

3. Confirmation

4. Ministration of Blessings

5. Commissioning for ministry

1. Impartation

There is an actual impartation from the administrator to the recipient

When a spirit filled anointed servant of God lays hands on a person, there is an impartation of Spiritual vitality; the life force of Elohim.

Natural man cannot impart spiritual power except through counterfeit demonic power from Satanic origin if the person is under the power of those influences.

It is impossible to impact that which you do not personally possess.

A believer must be spirit-filled and must be anointed for the ministry to be laying hands on people.

A believer must be tested and proved before they are allowed to minister to people at the church altar.

2. Identification

In the sacrificial system of the old testament there was an identification of the offerer with the sacrificial victim by means of physical contact.

"By the laying on of hands the offerer and the offering became one." Lev.1:4; Num 8:12.

Tim 5:22 warns regarding laying hands on another hastily; some people's sins are openly known others are secret. By laying hands, complete identification is made with the person and all that they are; therefore, you become partakers of their sins. This is why we need to be careful.

3. Confirmation

Confirming people in their gifting's and ministries. Acts 15:3; Acts 15:41.

Ordaining of Elders 1 Tim 4:14; 2 Tim 1:6, 14.

4. Ministration of Blessings

Laying on of hands or lifting hands towards another was done in an intent of blessing the people. Gen 48:13-20; Lev 9:22; Mk 10:13,16; Matt 19:13-15.

5. Commissioning of Ministry

This is an established practice in the ordination of ministry and in commissioning and sending forth of ministry. Acts 6:1-7.

Ordination of Timothy 1 Tim 4:14; 2 Tim 1:6.

Sending forth of Ministry Acts 13:3.

Hebrew Roots. The original foundation, Laying Hands Hebraic – Wikibooks, Google Search.

https://en.m.wikibooks.org/wiki/Hebrew_R oots/The_original_foundation/laying_Hands _Hebraic

Usurping Authority, What Does it Mean?

1. Seize and take control without authority and possibly with force; take as one's right or possession

2. Take the place of the pastor or leader without permission

We need to understand that the army of the Lord cannot afford to break rank, to know our place and boundaries. We need to learn to exercise self-control or be self-disciplined.

Can a church member correct a Church Leader? Would they be usurping authority?

I believe that there is no one in the church

who is above correction.

There is nothing wrong with approaching the pastor (leader) privately to tell them that you believe they made a mistake and especially if it's a doctrinal error. For petty issues it is always best to pray for your leader rather than being confrontational.

It is hoped that most pastors, since they too are capable of making mistakes, would be open to the idea that they gave out wrong information but the church or even church members have the obligation to correct a pastor where he is wrong in doctrinal positions.

No one is above correction because only the Word of God is perfect and no man is nor ever will be until we see him face to face.

Due to the lack of understanding in this issue many preachers have erred not having anyone to speak to them about their errors. The truth of the gospel has been slowly eroded due to error which went unchallenged which later became accepted doctrine. We all have an obligation to preserve the truth.

However, one needs wisdom in approaching an elder to point out the mistakes they have made. Look at Prophet Nathan when approaching King David about his sin with Bathsheba (2 Samuel 12). Nathan approached David with respect due to a King but was determined to ensure David was made aware of his sin. It is often the approach which determines whether your attempt is accepted or not. Also one needs to make sure you got your facts correct before approaching an elder or leader with an accusation.

"How much authority should a pastor have over a church?"

The church is called "the flock of God" (1 Peter 5:2), "God's heritage" (1 Peter 5:3), and "the church of God" (Acts 20:28). Jesus is "the head of the church" (Ephesians 5:23) and "the chief Shepherd" (1 Peter 5:4). The church rightly belongs to Christ, and He is the authority over it (Matthew 16:18). This is just as true of the local church as of the universal Body of Christ.

God's blueprint for building His church includes using men in the fivefold ministry of which pastor is one of them. The pastor is first an elder, and, along with the other elders, the pastor is responsible to do the following:

1. Oversee the church (1 Timothy 3:1). The primary meaning of the word bishop is "overseer." The general oversight of the ministry and operation of the church is the responsibility of the pastor and the other elders. This would include the handling of finances within the church (Acts 11:30).

2. Rule over the church (1 Timothy 5:17). The word translated "rule" literally means "to stand before." This would include the responsibility to exercise church discipline and reprove those who err from the faith (Matthew 18:15–17; 1 Corinthians 5:11–13).

3. Feed the church (1 Peter 5:3). Literally, the word pastor means

"shepherd." The pastor has a duty to "feed the flock" with God's Word and to lead them in the proper way.

4. Guard the doctrine of the church (Titus 1:9). The teaching of the apostles was to be committed to "faithful men" who would teach others also (2 Timothy 2:2). Preserving the integrity of the gospel is one of the pastor's important duties.

Having the full fivefold ministry in the church is very important for the perfecting (maturing) of the saints. One ministry alone e.g. pastor or evangelist is not enough, there is need of the apostle, the prophet and teacher even if they are mobile ministries as they bring balance to the body.

AMEN

THE BALM OF GILEAD WORLD MINISTRIES

Balm of Gilead World Ministries was started in 1996 by Merica and Joel Cox in Bulawayo, Zimbabwe for the Glory of God.

The family had returned to Zimbabwe from Zambia where they had served as missionaries and the church began in their family home in North End. The first service was attended by 15 people and three months later the meetings moved to a college hall in Lobengula Street. The church continued to grow and six months later the meetings moved again to the bigger hall at the Academy of Music.

The name Balm of Gilead comes from Jeremiah chapter 8 verse 22, "Is there no Balm in Gilead, is there no physician there? Why then is not the health of the daughter of my people recovered?

The Balm of Gilead logo came to Merica in a vision which she saw a rainbow, inscribed with the words "What is your hearts desire?". She answered, "To be like Jesus and to do the works which Jesus did, even greater works" and then saw a cloud ascending and lifting the rainbow higher into the sky. Merica chose the rainbow as a reminder of what she felt was a covenant with God, just as God made a covenant with Noah and gave him a rainbow for a sign.

In 2001, Merica came to the United Kingdom and settled in High Wycombe, starting a church in her lounge. The group later moved to Green Street Community Centre, again to the Reggie Grove Centre and then to the Wye Valley Community Centre as the size and popularity of the church grew and grew.

Since establishing that first church in High Wycombe, Merica has grown the church to meet demand with services in, Romford, Northampton and most recently Manchester

We thank the Lord for his faithfulness and pray he will use this ministry as a tool in His Hand for His Glory.

You can learn more about the Balm of Gilead World Ministries at our website:

www.bogministries.org

info@bogministries.org

JER 8:22
BALM OF GILEAD
WORLD MINISTRIES